Favorite Bible Stories

~This book belongs to~

....

Favorite
Bible Stories

Stories retold by
Libby Purves

Illustrated by
Eric Thomas

FAMILY LEARNING

FAMILY LEARNING

Project Editor Lee Simmons
Senior Editor Susan Peach
US Editor Kristin Ward
Art Editor Peter Radcliffe
Additional Design Sheilagh Noble

Managing Art Editor Chris Scollen
Managing Editor Jane Yorke
Production Josie Alabaster
DTP Designer Almudena Díaz
Jacket Design Adrienne Hutchinson

Religious Consultants Donald Kraus, Jenny Nemko,
Rt. Rev. Dom Stephen Ortiger, Jonathan Sharples

First American Edition, 1998
2 4 6 8 10 9 7 5 3 1

Published in the United States by
DK Publishing, Inc.
95 Madison Avenue
New York, NY 10016

Visit us on the World Wide Web at http://www.dk.com

Copyright © 1998 Dorling Kindersley Limited, London

Text copyright © 1998 Libby Purves

Published in Great Britain by Dorling Kindersley Limited.

Library of Congress cataloging is available upon request
ISBN 0-7894-2064-3

Color reproduction by Dot Gradations, Essex
Printed and bound in Italy by Mondadori

CONTENTS

The Old Testament

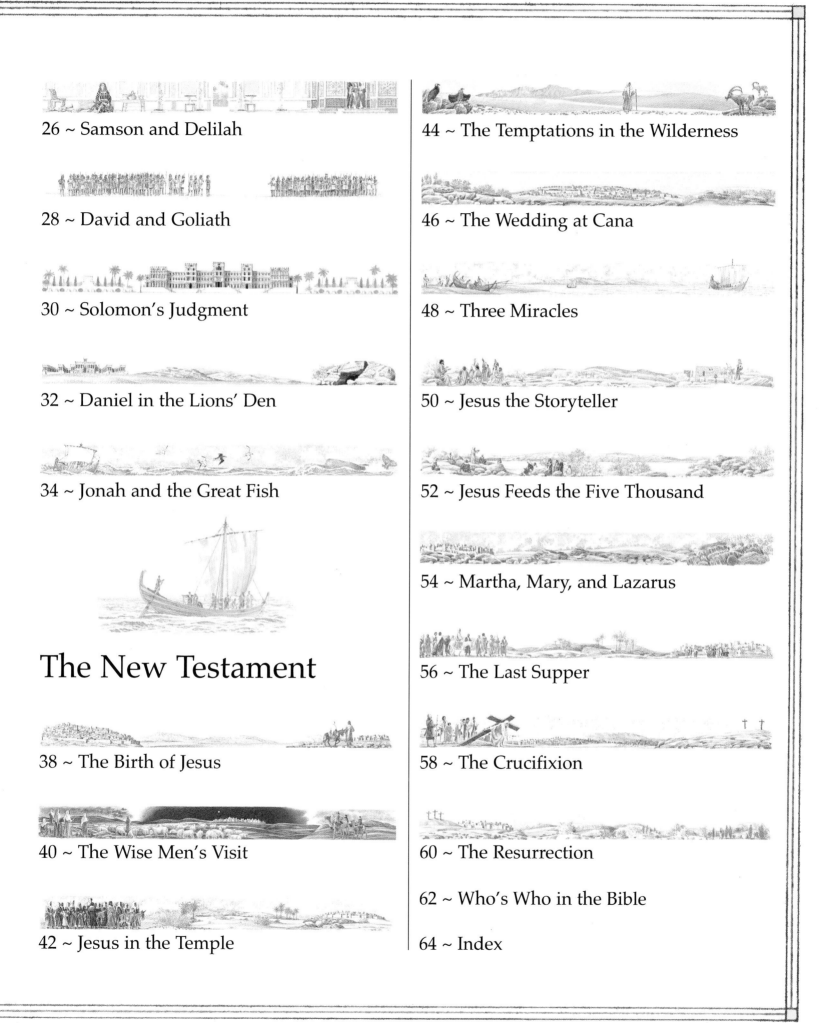

Introduction

EVERY CHILD SHOULD KNOW THE STORIES OF THE BIBLE. Not only are they some of the best stories ever told, but they have been central to Western culture for over a thousand years, and echoes of them run through our greatest literature, music, and art. A child is deprived who does not know about Joseph's coat, Solomon's judgment, the crossing of the Red Sea, and the birth of God's own son in a bare stable.

Seen in the light of Christian faith, of course, all these are far more than stories, but children can begin by reading them simply as adventures. Indeed, the Bible is above all a great adventure – the long, turbulent story of God's dealings with the creatures He made in His image, and how He gave them free will so that they could choose between good and evil.

Inevitably, because of that freedom they are not soft, reassuring stories. All human history and human life is riddled with conflict and violence, and both the Old and New Testaments are alive with it. Although the faithfulness of God to Man is the underlying theme of them all, the narratives of the Bible tell of terrible things; frightening violent events, suffering and treachery, defiance and defeat. Punishments are hard – the great Flood drowned the world, lions ate Daniel's false accusers, Jonah

suffered for his rebelliousness. Wickedness runs high; Cain kills Abel, Joseph's brothers throw him in a pit to die, the child Jesus is pursued by a king who kills all male newborn babies in the search for him, and the adult Jesus is betrayed by his friends.

These things may well frighten and alarm young children. I have tried to stay true to the biblical narration, and tell the stories honestly, but also to set them in the context of the wider, wonderful story of God's dealings with humankind. I have also tried to represent the fact that many of them have strong elements of humor – the humor of human incongruity and frailty.

Above all, they are rich stories, rich with images and symbols that strike deep into human hearts at any age, and belong to us all: the garden of Eden, the pairs of living creatures going trustfully into the Ark as the dark rain falls, the hush of Creation, the starlit night of the Nativity, the loving abundance of the loaves and fishes.

A young child cannot be expected to take in the whole Bible, but I hope that through this selection of interwoven, simply retold stories, those who read with children may begin to offer them the beginnings of an appreciation of the most extraordinary, inspiring, significant book the world has ever seen.

The Old Testament

GOD SAID, "I WILL MAKE PEOPLE TO LIVE IN
THIS WORLD. I WILL MAKE THEM LIKE ME,
TO LOVE AND CARE FOR MY CREATION."

On the first day, God says, "Let there be light!"

On the second day, God separates the sky from the sea.

On the third day, God creates land and all kinds of plants.

On the fourth day, God makes the Sun, the Moon, and the stars.

On the fifth day, God makes all the creatures of the sea and sky.

On the sixth day, God creates the animals and Adam and Eve.

On the seventh day, God rests.

God Makes the World

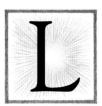

LONG, LONG AGO, AT THE BEGINNING OF TIME, GOD WAS ALL ALONE. THERE WAS JUST A GREAT, COLD, empty darkness. But by His great power, God made the Earth out of nothing, and it lay dark and covered in water.

Then God said, "Let there be light!" and there was light. And that was the first day.

On the second day, God made the sky, a wide, blue, shining arc above the water. But nothing moved, nothing was alive. God was still alone.

On the third day, God gave the Earth some shape. He gathered all the water neatly into one place, and left other parts dry. He gave names to these places – sea and land. On the land, He made grass grow and plants sprout up and open their leaves. He made trees and bushes and jungles, and forests, flowers, nuts and fruit. He made sure that there were seeds in the fruit, so that more plants and trees could grow year after year.

On the fourth day, God said, "Let there be lights in the sky to show the times and seasons!" And the warm Sun appeared by day, and the beautiful Moon and stars by night, and God was pleased.

On the fifth day, God made living things – birds to fly through the air, and fish, eels, starfish, corals, and all kinds of wriggling, swimming things to live in the sea. God blessed them all, and sent them on their way. "Go and lay plenty of eggs, so that there will be more of you to fill the sea and the sky!"

But there were still no animals on the land. So on the sixth day, God made cattle for the plains, monkeys and tigers for the jungle, big animals and small ones, strong ones and fluffy ones, rabbits to hop and snakes to creep, and even the tiniest, buzzing insects.

God creates all the animals and plants on Earth.

And then God did the greatest thing of all. He said, "I will make people to live in this world. I will make them like me, to love and care for my creation."

God made a man and a woman and named them Adam and Eve. He sent them out to explore the beautiful new world and told them to have babies, so that they and their children's children could fill the Earth, and farm it, and rule the animals wisely. God blessed Adam and Eve and told them to be good.

God looked around at everything He had made and was happy with what He saw. So on the seventh day, God rested. His work was done and He was pleased with it.

THE SEVENTH DAY IS CALLED THE SABBATH. GOD COMMANDED US TO USE IT AS A RESTFUL, HOLY DAY TO THINK OF HIM AND GIVE THANKS FOR THE WORLD. IN THE JEWISH RELIGION, SATURDAY IS THE SABBATH; FOR CHRISTIANS, IT IS SUNDAY.

Adam and Eve

 OD MADE A HOME FOR ADAM AND EVE — A GARDEN IN THE EAST, CALLED EDEN. A RIVER RAN through Eden, and the rocks sparkled with jewels. The grass was soft and there were cool, shady trees, bright, colorful flowers, and gentle animals. Every kind of fruit grew there and there was plenty for Adam and Eve and the animals to eat.

In this Paradise, Adam and Eve had no worries. The garden was warm, so they did not need clothes or shoes. They explored, tried new fruits, and looked after the animals God had put in their care. Sometimes God, their friend and master, came to talk with them.

In the center of the garden God put a tree, and He called it the Tree of the Knowledge of Good and Evil. Of course, Adam and Eve did not know about evil or violence, or death; none of these things had come into the world yet. All they knew about was the kindness of God and of each other, and the goodness of the Earth and the animals.

There was only one rule. God told them, "Eat any fruit that grows in the garden, but do not eat the fruit of the Tree of the Knowledge of Good and Evil or you will die."

Adam and Eve heard and understood, and for a while they obeyed God and lived in peace.

Eve was tempted by the serpent to taste the forbidden fruit from the Tree of Knowledge. Adam ate it, too.

But in the garden there was a cunning creature. It was the serpent. One day it found Eve and said, "I thought you were in charge of this garden."

"We are," said Eve proudly. "Isn't it beautiful?"

The snake stared at her with its cold, beady eyes. "Well," it said. "I hear that there is one tree you're not in charge of. You're not even allowed to eat the fruit."

"That's right," Eve replied. "We're allowed to eat any fruit at all, except from the Tree of the Knowledge of Good and Evil. God has forbidden us to touch it. We might die if we did."

The serpent laughed at her, a nasty, sneering, hissing laugh that made Eve feel angry, but strangely, a little silly, too.

"Nonsense!" the snake said. "God's lying. You won't die from it. The reason God won't let you eat that fruit is that if you *did*, you'd be as wise as He is. You'd know everything; all about Good and Evil, and all the things He knows. You'd be gods yourselves. Just as good as Him. That's why He doesn't want you to have it."

That made Eve really want to try the fruit. She wanted to know as much as God, and the fruit did look very tasty. She reached out and picked one from the Tree, and took a bite. Then she gave it to Adam, and he ate some of it, too.

Adam and Eve had done the only forbidden thing in the whole world. All at once they felt ashamed and

When Adam and Eve realized they were naked, they were ashamed and tried to hide from God.

embarrassed and wanted to hide themselves. They realized that they were naked, and for the first time they felt shy, so they sewed clothes out of fig leaves and clothed themselves.

That evening, when God came to walk in the garden in the cool of the evening, they were scared and hid from Him among the trees.

"Where are you?" called God.

Adam came out. "I heard your voice, and I was afraid because I am naked."

"Who told you that you were naked?" asked God. Have you been eating the forbidden fruit from the Tree of Knowledge?"

"It was Eve's fault," said Adam. "She gave it to me."

"It was the serpent's fault," said Eve. "He told me to." But they both knew that it was their own fault really.

God cursed the serpent. "You shall be the lowest of animals and the enemy of mankind. From now on, you will creep on your belly and eat dust. People will hate you forever and you will hate them."

Then God sadly told Adam and Eve, "You disobeyed my command, and now you must find out the difference between Good and Evil. Your life will change. I made you so you would be happy in this Paradise, but now you will have to work hard in the hot sun and scratch in the bare earth to grow your food. You will grow old and ill, and have sorrows, and one day you will die and become nothing but dust yourselves."

And as the sky went dark that evening, God drove Adam and Eve out of Eden, dressed in the skins of animals, to make their way in the world.

Hand in hand, walking slowly and sadly, they left their home in Paradise. At the gate of the garden God put an angel with a flaming sword to keep them out forever.

Adam and Eve were banished from Paradise for their disobedience.

GOD DID NOT MAKE ADAM AND EVE LIKE ROBOTS, WITH NO WILL OF THEIR OWN. THEY WERE FREE TO CHOOSE WHETHER TO OBEY HIM OR NOT. WHEN THEY DISOBEYED, THEY LOST PARADISE AND HAD TO LIVE WITH EVIL AND SUFFERING, AS WELL AS GOOD AND HAPPINESS.

God tells Noah to build a great ark before the rain comes.

Two animals of every kind are put on board.

As the rain falls, the ark floats higher and higher, until the flood covers the whole Earth.

As the waters subside, Noah sends a raven to look for land, but it soon returns.

Noah sends out a dove, and it returns with an olive leaf.

The flood is finally over. God promises never to deluge the Earth again.

Noah's Ark

 OUT IN THE WIDE WORLD, FAR FROM EDEN, ADAM AND EVE WORKED HARD FOR THEIR LIVING AND HAD borne children. But anger and wickedness had come into the world. Adam and Eve's son, Cain, even killed his own brother, Abel.

The descendants of Adam and Eve began to fill the world, and wickedness spread everywhere. God wished He had never made mankind, and decided to wash the world clean with a great flood.

There was only one good man, named Noah, who loved God. He and his wife had three sons, Ham, Shem, and Japheth, and each son had a wife of his own. God spoke to Noah, saying, "The world has grown very wicked, and I am going to destroy all the people and creatures I have made, except your family. You must build a ship, an ark, with a roof and three decks . . ." God gave Noah very strict instructions on how to build the ark, and ordered him to fill it with animals. "Find one male and one female of every creature," He ordered. "Cattle, snakes, insects, birds, everything that flies and walks and creeps on the Earth. When you are all aboard, I will make it rain for forty days."

Noah and his family did exactly as they were told. They collected animals, male and female of every kind, and labored to build the great ark. When everything was ready, the rain came. It beat on the roof of the ark, and as the water rose it floated the great ship off the ground. The water rose higher and higher, swirling and rocking the ark, until it reached the treetops, then the mountaintops, and the whole Earth was covered with water. The ark seemed very small. Inside, the family fed the animals and prayed and waited.

After a long, long time, the water finally started to subside, and the ark came to rest on the mountains of Ararat. Noah sent out a raven to look for land, but it came back because there was no dry place for it to rest. Then Noah sent out a dove, but it came back to the ark, too.

Seven days later, Noah sent the dove out again. This time it came back with a leaf from an olive tree in its beak. Then Noah knew that the water must be receding. The next time he sent the dove out, it didn't return. Noah realized it must have found a dry place to build a nest. When he looked out of the ark, he saw that the ground was beginning to dry. The flood was finally over.

God told Noah and his family to leave the ark and rule the world and its creatures wisely. He placed a rainbow in the sky and said, "This is a sign that I will never send such a flood again. Every time the rainbow appears, I will remember my promise to you and to all living creatures."

God saves Noah's family so they can go out into the world and start again.

GOD WAS PLEASED WITH NOAH. HE CHOSE TO SAVE NOAH AND HIS FAMILY BECAUSE OF NOAH'S TRUST IN HIM. AFTER THE FLOOD, GOD MADE MANKIND A PROMISE THAT HE WOULD NOT BRING SUCH A DISASTER TO THE EARTH AGAIN.

Jacob gives his favorite son, Joseph, a beautiful coat.

Joseph dreams of eleven sheaves of corn that bow down to him ...

... and the Sun, Moon, and stars as well.

Joseph's brothers are angry and jealous, and decide to kill him.

Reuben calls out to his brothers not to kill Joseph, but to throw him in a pit instead.

While Reuben is away, the brothers sell Joseph as a slave.

The brothers tell Jacob that Joseph is dead.

Joseph's Dreams

JACOB WAS A FARMER IN THE LAND OF CANAAN. HE HAD TWELVE SONS. BUT THE SON HE loved best was young Joseph. All the brothers worked hard, but Jacob hardly noticed the older ones. He gave Joseph a beautiful, striped coat of many colors, because Joseph was his favorite.

Of course this made the other brothers jealous. They couldn't bear the sight of Joseph in his fine coat. They were even angrier when he told them about a strange dream.

"Last night," Joseph said, "I dreamed that we were all tying up sheaves of corn in the fields at harvest time. My sheaf stood up straight, but all your sheaves bent over as if they were bowing to it!"

"What?" gasped the brothers. "Us, bow down to you?" They glared at him angrily.

Then Joseph had another dream. He said, "I dreamed that the Sun and Moon and eleven stars all bowed down to me." Even Jacob thought this was a little much – imagine suggesting that his mother and father should bow down to Joseph as well as his brothers!

The brothers truly hated Joseph now. One day, full of anger, they took their father's sheep to a distant field. Jacob had no idea how

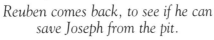

Reuben comes back, to see if he can save Joseph from the pit.

dangerously angry they were. He sent Joseph out to join them. When the brothers saw Joseph in his colored coat coming down the road, they said, "Here comes the dreamer! Let's kill him and throw him in a pit. We can pretend a wild animal got him."

But one brother, Reuben, had a kind heart. "No," he said. "Let's just throw Joseph in a pit and leave him." He planned to creep back later and rescue Joseph. Then Reuben left them for a while.

When Joseph arrived, the brothers tore off his coat and threw him in a pit. But, that evening, a group of Ishmaelites came past on camels. They were traveling merchants on their way to Egypt with cinnamon, and pepper, and precious spices. This gave Judah an idea. He said, "Let's sell Joseph to them as a slave. Then we won't have killed our own brother, but we'll still be rid of him." So they sold Joseph to the merchants for twenty pieces of silver. And when poor Reuben crept back to the pit to set his brother free, there was nobody there. He was horrified.

The brothers dipped Joseph's coat in goat's blood and took it home to show their father. "He must have been killed by a wild animal!" said Jacob, and he wept and tore his clothes in grief. For many days nobody could comfort him because he thought his dearest son was dead.

JOSEPH'S DREAMS WERE A GIFT FROM GOD, SENT TO PREPARE HIM FOR HIS ROLE IN THE FUTURE. HIS BROTHERS COULDN'T UNDERSTAND THIS BECAUSE THEY WERE JEALOUS OF THE SPECIAL PLACE THAT JOSEPH HAD IN JACOB'S HEART.

Joseph in Egypt

 **W**HEN THE ISHMAELITES GOT TO EGYPT, THEY SOLD JOSEPH TO AN ARMY CAPTAIN, NAMED Potiphar. Joseph worked hard, and soon Potiphar made him the chief servant of his household.

Joseph was a handsome young man, and Potiphar's wife took a fancy to him. "No," said poor Joseph, again and again. "Your husband trusts me, and it would be a sin to betray him." But the woman kept pestering him even though Joseph always said no. In the end, she took her revenge; she told Potiphar that Joseph had attacked her. The captain believed his wife's lies and threw Joseph into prison.

Even in prison, Joseph was helpful and made friends. He was especially good at telling people the meaning of their dreams because God had given him the gift of understanding. One of the people Joseph helped was a servant of Pharaoh, King of Egypt. When the servant was set free, he went back to work for Pharaoh and forgot about Joseph. But two years later he remembered him.

It was when Pharaoh began to have strange dreams. One night, he dreamed he was standing by the great Nile River. Seven fat cows came out of the river to graze. Then seven thin cows came out of the river and ate the fat cows, but did not grow fat themselves. The Pharaoh woke up, shuddering with fear.

When he fell asleep again, he dreamed of seven plump golden ears of corn growing on a single stalk. Suddenly seven, small, shriveled ears of corn sprouted and swallowed up the fat ones so that there was no good corn left.

These were powerful dreams, and it was a terrible night for Pharaoh. In the morning, pale and frightened, he called together the wisest men in Egypt to ask what these nightmares could possibly mean. Nobody knew. Then the servant who had been in prison said, "There's a prisoner named Joseph you could ask, a Hebrew from Canaan. He understands dreams. He got mine right."

"Get him!" ordered Pharaoh.

So Joseph stood alone before the great Pharaoh of Egypt. But he was not afraid, because he knew that God would guide him.

"God has sent these dreams to you," he said. "They mean that Egypt is going to have seven years of good harvests, with food to spare. Then there will be seven terrible years of famine, when nothing will grow. In the time of plenty you must save up all the grain you can for the bad years ahead."

Pharaoh believed Joseph and trusted him. He gave him a gold chain and ring, and said, "You will take charge of the harvest, and be the highest minister in Egypt after me."

Joseph did the job so well

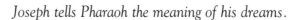

Joseph tells Pharaoh the meaning of his dreams.

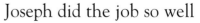

Joseph's brothers come to beg for food. They bow down before Joseph, but do not recognize him.

that there was plenty of food for everyone in the famine years. But in his old homeland in Canaan, there was little food and his family was starving. After two years Jacob was desperate. He sent ten of Joseph's brothers to Egypt to try to buy corn. His youngest son, Benjamin, stayed at home to keep him company.

When the brothers got to Pharaoh's court they bowed down to the chief minister without recognizing that it was Joseph.

Joseph decided to test them. He pretended not to know who they were. He called them spies, and put them in prison for three days so that they could see what it was like to be helpless and far from home.

Then he asked them if they had another brother. When they told him about Benjamin, he ordered that one of them stay behind as a hostage, while the others

fetched him. The brothers felt guilty, and wondered whether this was a punishment for the way they had treated Joseph. Joseph felt sorry for them, but went on with his plan.

When they brought Benjamin, Joseph filled their sacks with corn, and in Benjamin's he hid a silver cup. As they were leaving the city, he told the guards to search their sacks. They found the cup, and Joseph pretended to be angry. He said he would keep the thief as a slave.

At this, the brothers begged for mercy. "Keep me as a slave instead," said Judah. "Our poor father has already lost his favorite son, Joseph. To lose Benjamin would kill him."

Joseph saw that Judah and his other brothers had learned kindness, and were better men than they used to be. His heart was filled with love.

"I am Joseph," he said. "But don't be afraid. Don't even be sorry that you sold me as a slave all those years ago. It was God's will that I should come here to save lives in the years of famine. Tell our father, Jacob, that you can all come and live here in Egypt with me."

Joseph hugged them and wept for joy, and everything was forgiven. Jacob and all his sons and their wives made their home in Egypt, and for many years they and their descendants lived there in peace.

Joseph tells the guards to search the brothers' sacks. They find the stolen cup in Benjamin's sack.

THE TWELVE SONS OF JACOB WERE THE FATHERS OF THE TWELVE GREAT TRIBES OF ISRAEL. IN SPITE OF THE BROTHERS' CRIME, GOD'S PLAN BROUGHT THE FAMILY SAFELY BACK TOGETHER TO BE THE FOUNDERS OF THE ISRAELITES.

The Egyptians make the Israelites their slaves.

Pharaoh orders that all Israelite baby boys must be killed.

One mother hides her baby in a basket by the river.

Pharaoh's daughter finds the baby among the bulrushes.

The baby's sister comes forward and offers to find a nurse for him.

She runs to tell her mother the baby is safe.

Moses goes to live with the Princess in the royal palace.

Moses in the Bulrushes

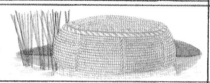

 ANY YEARS AFTER JOSEPH'S TIME, LIFE BECAME BITTERLY HARD FOR THE ISRAELITES IN EGYPT. THE EGYPTIANS treated them as slaves, beating them and forcing them to build roads and cities, and work hard in the fields. In spite of this, they were so healthy and strong that the Pharaoh of Egypt grew afraid. "There are too many Israelites!" he said angrily. "Suppose they began to fight us?"

So Pharaoh did the only thing he could think of, and a cruel thing it was, too. He ordered that every baby boy born to the Israelite slaves be drowned in the river.

However, one woman managed to hide her little son away for

An Israelite mother made a basket to hide her baby in.

three whole months. When at last it became too difficult to hide the baby, she knew she would have to give him up. Although she was sad and afraid, she still hoped to save him. In secret, she wove a basket out of reeds, made a lid for it, and smeared it with clay and tar to keep the water out. Then she laid the baby in the basket and left him alone, among the bulrushes on the banks of the Nile River.

The mother went sadly home, but the boy's older sister stayed nearby, watching – waiting to see what would happen to him. After a while, Pharaoh's daughter came down to bathe in the river. The sister hid, and watched. The Princess noticed the curious basket nestling among the bulrushes and said to her servants, "Bring it to me!" When the Princess opened the lid of the basket, the baby began to cry, and her heart was touched. She guessed that this must be one of the Israelite boys, who were doomed to die by her father's command.

While she was wondering what she could do to save him, the baby's sister crept up and said timidly, "The baby needs milk. Shall I find you a woman to nurse him?"

The Princess smiled. This was the answer to her problem. "Yes," she said. The girl ran to fetch her mother and they came back together. The Princess ordered the woman, "Nurse this baby for me while he is small, and I will pay you." So the mother got her own baby back, he was safe, and the Princess paid her wages for looking after him.

When the boy was older, Pharaoh's daughter had him brought to her. She adopted him, giving him a new name, Moses, and he grew up in splendor in the royal palace. Although Moses was brought up as an Egyptian, he never forgot that he was the child of an Israelite slave.

Moses stayed with his mother until he was old enough to go to the palace.

WHEN MOSES GREW UP HE LEFT EGYPT AND WENT TO THE LAND OF MIDIAN. BUT GOD TOLD HIM TO GO BACK AND LEAD THE ISRAELITES OUT OF EGYPT TO FREEDOM AND A COUNTRY OF THEIR OWN – CANAAN, THE PROMISED LAND.

Water turns into blood.

Frogs plague the land.

Gnats sting the people.

Egyptian children die.

Flies swarm in the air.

Darkness falls like night.

Egyptian cattle die.

Pharaoh makes false promises.

Locusts devour the crops.

Hailstones flatten the crops.

Boils appear on people's skin.

The Ten Plagues

NE DAY, WHEN MOSES WAS GROWN UP, GOD SPOKE TO HIM.

HE TOLD MOSES TO LEAD THE ISRAELITES out of Egypt, where they were slaves, to live in the Promised Land, the land of Canaan.

So Moses and his brother, Aaron, went to Pharaoh, King of Egypt, with a message, "The Lord, the God of Israel, says 'Let My people go!'" But Pharaoh refused to listen. So, to show God's power, Aaron struck the Nile River with his stick. All the water turned into blood. For a week there was no water to drink and a terrible smell of dead fish. Yet Pharaoh still said no.

So Aaron raised his stick by the river banks, and millions of frogs hopped from the river, invading the houses and even the beds. Pharaoh hated the plague.

"Make your God take the frogs away!" he said. "Then you can go."

But Pharaoh broke his word. So Aaron struck the sand, and all the grains turned into stinging gnats. Everyone itched all over. Next came clouds of black, buzzing flies, which spoiled the food and got in people's eyes. Pharaoh began to change his mind. But as soon as the insects had gone, he refused to set the Israelites free.

God was angry; he sent a plague to kill the horses and cattle. Still Pharaoh wouldn't give in. Then Moses and

Aaron struck the ground with his stick, and terrible plagues came over the land of Egypt.

Aaron picked up handfuls of ashes and threw them in the air; wherever they landed, people got big, painful lumps on their skin, called boils. But Pharaoh was still stubborn.

So Aaron raised his hands to the sky and there came a great storm of hail and fire and thunder, smashing the trees and crops. Pharaoh was terrified. "Ask your God to stop it!" he said, "and I will let you go."

But as soon as the sun came out, he changed his mind. So God sent swarms of locusts, which ate all the corn and fruit and left the fields black and dead. Then God sent darkness for three whole days. At last Pharaoh agreed.

"You can go," he said, "But you must leave your sheep and cattle."

"No," said Moses. "We need them for the journey to the Promised Land." Pharaoh rudely turned his back.

Then God sent the worst plague of all.

"The firstborn, the eldest child of every house, shall die." he said. To keep the Israelites safe, he told them to kill a lamb for a meal that evening. "Put a mark on the door with the lamb's blood," he said. "And the plague will pass over you."

That terrible night, the firstborn child of every Egyptian family died, even Pharaoh's own child.

"Go," said Pharaoh, in grief. "Go, and serve your God, and may He forgive me."

So finally, the people of Israel gathered up their belongings and left Egypt forever.

EVERY YEAR JEWISH PEOPLE CELEBRATE PASSOVER WITH A SPECIAL SERVICE AND MEAL IN THEIR HOMES. THE STORY OF PASSOVER IS READ ALOUD TO RECALL THE TIME LONG AGO WHEN GOD SET THEIR ANCESTORS FREE FROM SLAVERY IN EGYPT.

By day, God leads the Israelites in a column of cloud.

By night, God leads them in a column of fire.

Pharaoh's army chases after the Israelites.

God sends a column of cloud to protect the Israelites.

By God's power, Moses parts the Red Sea.

The Red Sea flows back and the Egyptians are drowned. The Israelites are free at last!

The Crossing of the Red Sea

FTER THE ISRAELITES LEFT EGYPT THEY WALKED FOR MANY DAYS AND NIGHTS THROUGH desert and rocks and wilderness. God led the way; by day He came in a column of cloud, and by night in a column of fire. Sometimes the people became tired and hungry and afraid.

"We were all right in Egypt," they said angrily to Moses. "Why did you bring us out here to die in the wilderness?"

"God will protect us," said Moses. "He will lead us to the Promised Land, where there will be food and shelter, milk and honey, and we shall be free. Have faith!"

Meanwhile, back in Egypt, Pharaoh had forgotten the lesson he had learned, and lost his temper again.

"Why did I let those Israelite slaves go?" he raged. "We need them to do all the work!" So he set out with a great army of soldiers to get them back.

When they saw the distant army approaching, with chariots and horses, swords and armor, the Israelites were camped on the shore of the Red Sea. They were footsore and weary, and did not know what to do. They had no boats, and were trapped between a furious army and the sea.

There was no way that they could escape. But Moses said, "Do not fear."

Just then, a great pillar of cloud, sent by God, covered the Egyptian army so that they were confused and in darkness. The Israelites could still see clearly.

Then Moses stretched his hand out over the sea. A great wind sprang up from the east. The waters of the sea rose up with a roar and parted. The Israelites looked, and suddenly saw that there was a path, a dry path, lying ahead of them through the sea.

Moses led his people along that strange path through the sea; they walked on the seabed with water on either side of them rising like high, green walls.

When the Egyptians saw what was happening, they tried to follow the escaping Israelites along the path. But God told Moses to stretch out his hand again. And the waters closed over the Egyptians and drowned them all.

The Israelites arrived safely on the other side and climbed up the far shore of the Red Sea to make their camp.

The Israelites camped by the shores of the Red Sea.

Miriam, the sister of Moses and Aaron, took her tambourine and began to dance for joy. There, on the seashore, she led the Israelites dancing and singing, to praise God for their safe passage across the sea, and for the end of their long years of slavery in Egypt.

THE ISRAELITES TRAVELED FOR FORTY YEARS. GOD LOOKED AFTER THEM AND GAVE THEM LAWS. THE MOST IMPORTANT ONES ARE CALLED THE TEN COMMANDMENTS. HE KEPT THE ISRAELITES SAFE, UNTIL AT LAST THEY REACHED THE PROMISED LAND.

Samson, the strongest man in Israel, fights the Philistines.

The Philistines ask Delilah to find out the secret of Samson's strength.

Delilah ties Samson with bowstrings, then ropes, but he breaks them.

She tries to weave Samson's hair into her loom, but he breaks free again.

The secret is in Samson's hair. While he sleeps, his enemies cut it off and his power is gone.

Samson is blinded and thrown into prison.

God gives Samson back his strength for one last time.

Samson destroys the temple and everyone in it.

Samson and Delilah

**S**AMSON WAS THE STRONGEST MAN IN ISRAEL. BEFORE HE WAS BORN, GOD HAD DECIDED THAT HE WOULD use Samson to free the Israelites from their enemies, the Philistines. An angel told Samson's mother that, to show he trusted in God for his strength, Samson must never cut his hair.

Samson grew up tall and strong. He fought hard in many battles, and won great victories with God's help. When he was older, he fell in love with a woman named Delilah. She seemed to love him, but the Philistine lords came to her in secret and said, "Find out the secret of your man's strength so that we can defeat him. We will pay you with many pieces of silver."

Delilah tried. Prettily, she asked Samson, "How can you be so strong? Isn't there anything that could capture you?"

Samson teased her. "If I were tied up with seven brand-new bowstrings, I would be helpless," he said. So Delilah tied him up, as if it were a joke, then shouted, "Help! the Philistines are coming!" Samson jumped up, snapping the strings easily.

Delilah tried again. This time Samson told her that only new ropes could hold him; but he broke those ropes as easily as a spider's web. Next time he said, "Weave my hair into your loom, then I will lose my strength." Delilah tried that, but when she cried, "Philistines!" Samson easily pulled his hair out of her loom.

Delilah cried and nagged and pestered. "You don't love me!" she said. "You keep telling me lies! You're making fun of me!"

At last Samson was worn out with her wailing, and he told her the truth. "If my hair were cut," he said, "The strength that God gives me would be lost."

One day, while Samson was asleep, resting his head on her lap, Delilah called his enemies in to cut off his hair. When Samson woke up, all his strength had left him. The Philistines bound him and blinded him, then threw him in prison.

But slowly, Samson's hair grew back. One day, the Philistines held a great celebration in their temple to thank their god Dagon for their luck in capturing Samson. "Bring him out!" shouted the people. "Let's see him!"

Samson was led out. He stood between the pillars of the great temple, and while the crowd laughed and mocked, he prayed, "Oh, Lord God, give me back my strength, just once more!"

Then Samson put his hands on the massive pillars and pushed. At that moment, God gave him back his strength. With a great crack and a rumble, the temple fell down, and the Philistines were killed. Samson died too, but he had won his last great victory.

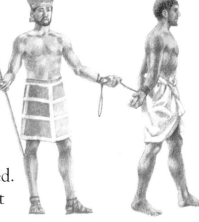
Samson is bound and led out into the temple.

SAMSON KNEW HE SHOULD NOT TRUST DELILAH WITH THE SECRET TO HIS STRENGTH, WHICH BELONGED TO GOD, BUT HE GAVE IN TO HER. WHEN HE WAS WEAK AND BLIND HE HAD ONLY GOD TO RELY ON, AND HIS TRUST IN GOD GAVE HIM BACK HIS STRENGTH.

The Philistine army.

The Israelite army.

Every day, the Philistine Goliath taunts the Israelite army.

Goliath shouts his challenge to the Israelites.

David offers to fight Goliath, but his brothers tell him to leave.

King Saul offers David his armor.

With a single shot from his sling, David hits Goliath.

Goliath is dead!

Alone, David faces Goliath.

Goliath falls to the ground.

The battle is won.

David and Goliath

DAVID WAS A SHEPHERD BOY, AND WATCHED HIS FATHER'S FLOCKS ON THE HILLS ABOVE Bethlehem. But God had chosen him to be a future great leader. Until then David lived at home and looked after the sheep, and in the long, starry nights he would play his harp.

Saul, the King, was sad and restless. He heard of the young shepherd's music. "Send me this boy," he said. David came and played to him, and when the King's bad mood went away David went back home to his sheep.

But the King had other troubles. A great army of Philistines had gathered on a hillside to wage war on the Israelites; a terrible battle was beginning. David's elder brothers were in the Israelite army, and one day their father, Jesse, sent David to them with bread and cheese and corn. When he arrived he found an uproar. The Philistines had a champion fighter, a huge man named Goliath of Gath. With his great brass helmet and heavy armor, he stood taller and broader and stronger than any man ever seen. Goliath was mocking the Israelites, and offering to end the war in one fight, man to man.

"I am one man!" he said. "Send me one of your soldiers! If any of you can kill me, the Philistines will be your servants.

Goliath of Gath, a giant of a man, fought in the Philistine army.

If I kill your champion, you can serve us!"

But all the Israelites were afraid of Goliath. David saw this, and said, "Who is this Philistine, who dares insult the armies of the living God?" His brothers were angry, and told David to get back to his sheep. But he went straight to see King Saul and said, "Israelites must not be afraid. I will fight Goliath."

"But you are only a boy," said the King.

David answered, "When a lion and a bear threatened my sheep, I killed them with God's help. God will help me now." King Saul offered David his armor and a sword, but they were too heavy for him. Instead, he stooped and picked up five, smooth stones. Then alone, with his sling, David walked toward the giant.

Goliath laughed. "I am not a dog, to be driven off by a boy! Come here, I'll feed you to the birds!"

But David said, "You may have a sword and spear, but I come against you in the name of the God of Israel, whom you have defied. Today He will hand you over to me."

He put a stone in his sling, swung it once, and sent it flying. It hit Goliath on his forehead, breaking his skull, and he fell. Then David took Goliath's sword and cut his head off. So the battle was won, and the Israelites rejoiced.

David was a young Israelite shepherd boy.

DAVID LATER BECAME A GREAT KING OF THE ISRAELITES, AND THE FATHER OF OTHER KINGS. THE NEW TESTAMENT TELLS US THAT BETHLEHEM, HIS HOME, BECAME THE BIRTHPLACE OF JESUS.

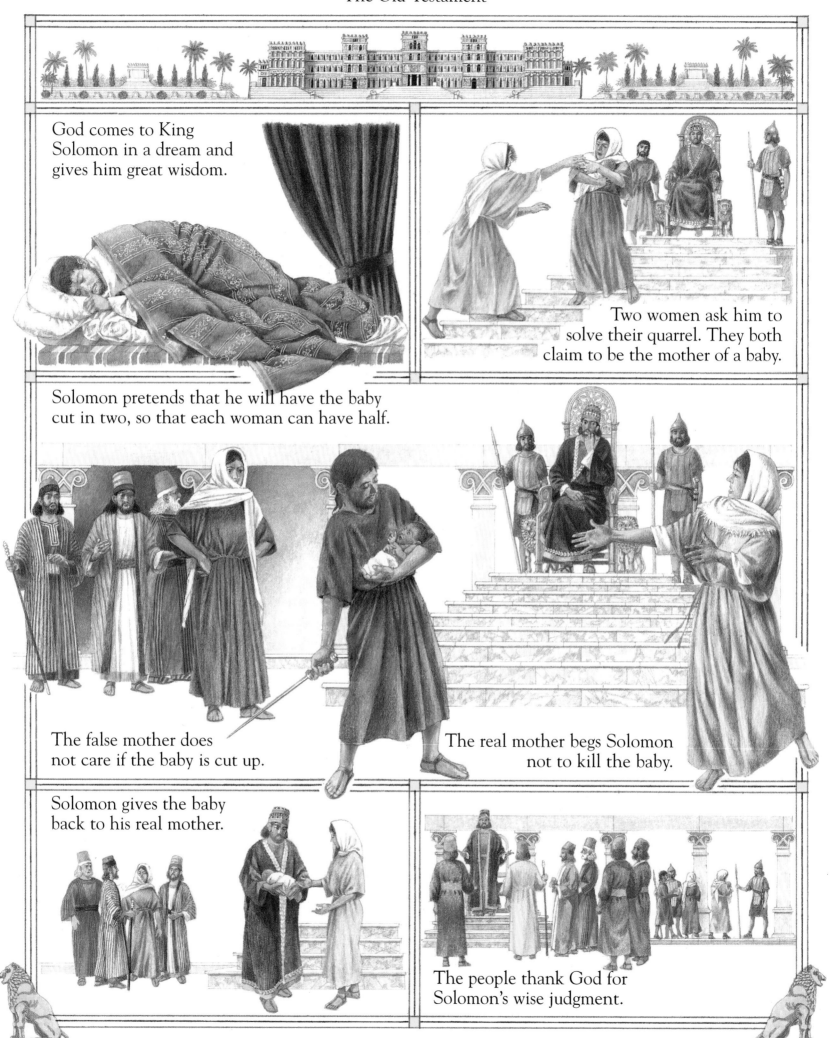

God comes to King Solomon in a dream and gives him great wisdom.

Two women ask him to solve their quarrel. They both claim to be the mother of a baby.

Solomon pretends that he will have the baby cut in two, so that each woman can have half.

The false mother does not care if the baby is cut up.

The real mother begs Solomon not to kill the baby.

Solomon gives the baby back to his real mother.

The people thank God for Solomon's wise judgment.

Solomon's Judgment

URING KING DAVID'S REIGN, ISRAEL HAD BECOME A GREAT KINGDOM. WHEN DAVID DIED, HIS young son Solomon became King of Israel in his place.

One night, God came to Solomon in a dream and said, "Ask for anything you want and I shall give it to you."

Solomon replied, "You helped my father David, and made him a great king of a great nation. Now, Lord, you have made me king instead of him. I feel like a little child. I know that I am not wise enough to rule Israel. So please, give me wisdom and an understanding heart, so that I will be able to tell what is right and what is wrong."

God was pleased. "You could have asked for long life, and riches, and victories, but instead you asked only for wisdom. Because of this, I will indeed make you wise, but you shall have great riches and honor as well, and live a long life, keeping my commandments."

Then Solomon woke from the dream. He thanked God and held a great feast.

His new wisdom was very soon tested. Two women came to King Solomon and asked him to settle their quarrel.

The first one said, "Lord King, we live in the same house. I had a baby, and two days later this woman had a baby, too. We were alone in the house, and her baby died in the night. She crept into my room and stole my baby, and put her dead child in my arms. Make her give my baby back to me!"

The other woman said, "No! The living baby is mine. It was her baby that died!"

Solomon had no way of telling which of the two mothers was lying. He thought for a while, then said to one of the servants, "Fetch a sword!"

The servant brought a sharp sword, while the women wondered what the King was going to do. Then Solomon said, "Cut the baby in half. Then the women can have half each!"

The false mother said angrily, "All right. Neither of us shall have him – cut the baby in half!"

But the real mother was shocked and terrified, and her heart went out to her baby. "No, no!" she cried. "Give him to this other woman. She can have him, only do not kill him!" She loved her baby so much that she would rather lose him forever than let him be killed.

King Solomon smiled. Now he knew who the real mother was. He said gently, "Do not hurt the baby. This is his mother. Give him back to her."

All of Israel heard the story of Solomon's first judgment and realized that such wisdom must be a gift from God.

A servant brings King Solomon a sword.

GOD KEPT HIS PROMISE. SOLOMON FOLLOWED IN KING DAVID'S FOOTSTEPS AND BECAME ONE OF THE GREAT KINGS OF ISRAEL. GOD USED SOLOMON TO BRING PEACE AND PROSPERITY, AND PEOPLE FROM ALL NATIONS CAME TO HEAR HIS WISE SAYINGS.

Daniel is the King's favorite, and this makes other officials jealous.

They persuade the King to ban praying.

Daniel continues to pray to God.

The jealous officials report Daniel to the King.

Reluctantly, the King has Daniel thrown to the lions.

Next morning, the King visits the lions' den.

God has protected Daniel and he is still alive!

The King declares that everyone should worship Daniel's God.

The wicked officials are thrown to the lions.

Daniel in the Lions' Den

THE ISRAELITES HAD BEEN DEFEATED IN WAR AND WERE RULED OVER BY THE KING OF BABYLON. THE KING, Darius, took some of the most clever Israelites to serve him, and one of these was Daniel. Like Joseph many years before, Daniel was wise and had the gift of understanding dreams. He grew to be one of the most powerful men in the kingdom, and yet he never forgot that he was an Israelite and must always pray to God.

But Daniel had enemies, other officials who were jealous of him. They thought of a clever way to get rid of him. They went to King Darius and said "O King, may you live forever!" and praised him as if he were a god. Then they persuaded the foolish king to make a law, saying that for thirty days nobody must pray to any god or man except to the King himself. Anybody caught praying to another god would be thrown into a den of lions.

Daniel ignored the rule, and went on praying to the true God three times a day. His enemies spied on him through the open window of his room. When they saw him praying, they ran to the king and said, "That Israelite Daniel does not respect you. He has ignored your law. He must be thrown to the lions."

King Darius saw that he had been tricked, and his heart was heavy. He wanted to save Daniel, but he knew that he must obey his own law. At last he agreed that Daniel should be thrown to the lions, but said to his friend, "May your God, the God you serve, rescue you." Then King Darius turned away to hide his grief, for the lions were very savage, and he was almost sure that Daniel would die.

So Daniel was pushed into the lions' den, and the entrance was sealed with a great stone. King Darius could not sleep that night, and would not eat. The next morning he ran to the den and cried out in grief, "Daniel, has the God you serve been able to save you from the lions?"

A voice came from the den. "King Darius! My God has sent his angel, and closed the mouths of the lions. They did not hurt me because I am innocent in God's sight. I have done you no harm, O King."

King Darius was very happy, and commanded that Daniel should be released. When he came out of the den, Daniel was calm and unhurt, and the people saw that God had saved him.

Then the King ordered that Daniel's enemies, who had tried to have him killed should be thrown to the lions themselves. So they were, and the lions killed them instantly.

After this, King Darius decreed that all through the kingdom, everybody should worship the God of Daniel, because He was a powerful and faithful God, who cared for His people.

The power of God makes the lions gentle.

THE STORY OF DANIEL SHOWS THAT IT IS GOD'S JUDGMENT THAT MATTERS, NOT MAN'S. ALTHOUGH DANIEL HAD BROKEN KING DARIUS'S LAW, HE WAS SAVED FROM THE LIONS BECAUSE HE HAD ALWAYS OBEYED GOD'S LAW.

God tells Jonah to preach in Nineveh, but he refuses.

Jonah runs away to sea.

God sends a storm to frighten Jonah.

Jonah tells the sailors the storm will stop if they throw him overboard.

A great fish comes and swallows Jonah whole.

Inside the fish, Jonah prays to God.

The fish throws Jonah onto the land.

Jonah preaches to the people of Nineveh and they repent.

Jonah shelters from the sun under a vine.

God teaches Jonah a lesson by killing the vine.

Jonah and the Great Fish

JONAH WAS ONE OF GOD'S PROPHETS; A SPECIAL MAN CHOSEN BY GOD TO TELL PEOPLE ABOUT HIS LAWS. One day, God told Jonah to go and preach in the city of Nineveh. The people there were very wicked and God wanted them to repent. Jonah did not want to go. He ran away and got on a ship sailing in the opposite direction.

God was angry. He sent a great storm, so that the ship almost broke apart in the waves. The sailors were terrified, and thought that someone on board must be cursed. The captain went to Jonah and said, "Pray to your God to save us!"

Jonah looked out at the storm and said, "It is my fault. I have brought this trouble and danger on you. I am an Israelite, and I serve the God who made the land and the sea. I have disobeyed Him and made Him angry. Throw me overboard and your ship will be safe."

They did not want to, but soon the storm became so bad that the sailors decided they must do it. "Forgive us, God," they said, and they took hold of Jonah and threw him into the sea. All at once, the water grew calm.

Jonah had hardly a moment to think before an enormous fish came and swallowed him up, whole. Jonah found that he was still alive, sitting in its belly. There he stayed, inside the fish, for three days and three nights; but Jonah never complained, only prayed and thanked God for saving him from death. At last the fish came near land and spat him onto the beach.

Again, God told Jonah to go to Nineveh. This time, Jonah did as he was told. He warned the people that in forty days, God would destroy their city because of their sinful ways. They listened to Jonah and were sorry. Even the King took off his rich robes and wore sackcloth, asking God to forgive the people of Nineveh. God heard their prayers and had mercy.

But Jonah sat outside the city, waiting for God to destroy it. He was angry when nothing happened. God watched over him, and made a vine grow up to shade him from the hot sun. Jonah stayed there, waiting to see the city burned and ruined. Still nothing happened.

The next day God sent a worm, which killed the vine. Jonah sweated in the hot sun and was even angrier. Then God said, "Why are you angry that the vine has withered? You don't seem to care about the thousands of people in Nineveh." So Jonah learned an important lesson about God's power and of God's forgiveness.

The people of Nineveh listen to Jonah's warning and are sorry for their wicked ways.

GOD GAVE JONAH A SECOND CHANCE TO DO WHAT HE HAD ASKED. BUT JONAH HAD TO LEARN THAT THE PEOPLE OF NINEVEH DESERVED A SECOND CHANCE TOO. GOD FORGAVE THEIR SINS, JUST AS HE WILL ALWAYS FORGIVE US WHEN WE ARE SORRY.

The New Testament

THIS MUST BE THE CHRIST, THE SAVIOR
WHO GOD HAD PROMISED WOULD COME
TO HELP HUMANKIND.

God sends the Angel Gabriel to tell Mary that she will have a son.

Mary visits her cousin Elizabeth to tell her the news.

An angel visits Joseph in a dream.

Joseph and Mary have to travel to Bethlehem.

Joseph and Mary search for a room.

Jesus is born in a stable.

Mary wraps Jesus up warmly and lays him in a manger.

The Birth of Jesus

TWO THOUSAND YEARS AGO, IN A SMALL TOWN CALLED NAZARETH IN THE LAND OF GALILEE, THERE lived a good, gentle young woman named Mary. She planned to marry a man named Joseph and live an ordinary, quiet life in Nazareth.

One day, however, an angel named Gabriel came to her and said, "The Lord is with you! You are the most blessed of women!"

Mary did not understand, but Gabriel told her not to be afraid. "God has chosen you to be the mother of His child. Your son shall be called Jesus, and be known as the Son of God."

"But how?" asked Mary. "I am not married!"

The angel told Mary that she would have the child through the power of the Holy Spirit. Mary knelt before the angel and bowed her head. "I am God's servant," she said. "Let His will be done."

She was full of wonder, and hurried away to visit her cousin Elizabeth. Elizabeth was expecting a baby too, and as Mary entered her house she felt it leap for joy inside her. She cried out, "You are the most blessed of women! Your child is holy!" Mary then praised the power of God, and the two women were filled with wonder, and felt the

Mary is a young woman from Nazareth.

presence of God all around them.

After a few months, Joseph saw that Mary was expecting a baby. He was bewildered, but the angel came to him, too, and said, "Do not worry; take Mary for your wife. Her son comes from God." So Mary and Joseph were married.

Joseph is engaged to marry Mary.

But just when Mary's baby was almost due, they had to set out on a long journey. The emperor Augustus had passed a law saying that everyone had to go back to the town where they had been born to be registered. All over the country people were traveling. Joseph was from Bethlehem in Judea, where the great King David had been born many centuries before. So Joseph and Mary traveled from Nazareth to the town of Bethlehem, and by the end of the journey Mary was very tired. She felt sure that her baby would be born soon.

The couple had nowhere to sleep. Every house and inn in Bethlehem was full. Joseph searched everywhere, but no one had room for them. At last they got permission to take shelter in a rough stable, among the animals. Here, on the straw, Mary's baby son was born. She wrapped him up carefully in strips of cloth and made him a bed in the manger that the animals used. There was nowhere else to put him. That night, tired and thankful, Mary and Joseph watched over the baby Jesus.

JESUS CHOSE TO COME DOWN FROM HEAVEN AND LIVE WITH US FOR A TIME AS A HUMAN. HE WAS BORN IN A POOR, COMFORTLESS PLACE — A SIGN THAT HE WOULD BE ON THE SIDE OF THE POOR AND THOSE WHO SUFFER.

The Wise Men's Visit

 **I**N THE HILLS ABOVE BETHLEHEM, THERE WERE SHEPHERDS SITTING AROUND CAMPFIRES THROUGH THE night, guarding their sheep from wolves and foxes and thieves.

Suddenly their tired eyes saw a brilliant glow in the sky lighting up the whole hillside around them. An angel appeared, so bright that they covered their eyes and trembled with fear.

But the angel said to the shepherds, "Do not be afraid. I bring you good news, joyful news for everyone in the world. Today, in Bethlehem, a child has been born, and he is Christ the Lord, the Savior of the World. You will find him there tonight, wrapped in strips of cloth and lying in a manger."

As the angel spoke, the light grew even brighter and suddenly the whole sky was filled with angels singing "Glory to God in the highest! Peace on Earth and goodwill to all men!"

The shepherds knew that this must be Christ, the Savior who God had promised would come to help humankind. When the angels had left, they got up and left their fires and their sheep to run down to the little town as fast as they could.

There they found Mary and Joseph, and saw baby

The shepherds see a brilliant light and an angel appears to tell them that Jesus has been born.

Jesus lying in the manger, just as the angel had said. The shepherds went away praising God and told everyone they met about the wonderful events they had seen and all that they had been told. Those who heard them were amazed. Mary stayed quietly with her baby, but deep in her heart she thought about these wonderful happenings.

Far away in the East, some wise men saw a new star shining in the sky. They knew that this meant a new king of the Jews had been born, so they traveled to Jerusalem to visit the king.

When they arrived they began asking everyone, "Where is this child? Where is this new king of the Jews? We have seen a wonderful new star in the East, that tells of his coming. We have come to worship him."

Herod, the king of Judea, heard about this and was afraid and angry. He was worried that this child they spoke of would be made king instead of him. He decided that he would have to kill the baby as soon as possible. But he had no idea where Jesus was. So he invited the wise men to his court and said craftily, "When you have found the child, please come back and tell me where he is. I would like to worship him, too."

The wise men saw the star again, and it seemed to be leading them. They followed it all the way to Bethlehem. The glowing star led them to the town, to the street, to the very house, stopping over

The wise men travel to Bethlehem to see Jesus, king of the Jews, bringing gifts of gold, frankincense, and myrrh.

the place where Mary, Joseph, and Jesus were.

The wise men entered the place. As soon as they saw Mary with the child, they bowed down before him and worshipped him. They gave Jesus rich gifts of gold, frankincense, and myrrh – presents fit for a king.

Then the wise men went away and rested after their travels. But while they slept, God spoke to them in their dreams, warning them not to go back to Herod because he wanted to kill Jesus. So the wise men quickly left Bethlehem, traveling home in secret by another route.

Later Joseph had a dream, too. An angel came to warn him about Herod's plan to murder Jesus. The angel told him to take Mary and the baby and escape over the

border into the land of Egypt, where Herod had no power. It would be a long and difficult journey through the great desert, but Joseph obeyed. That very night, in the darkness, he set out for Egypt with his sleepy wife and her baby.

Meanwhile, back in Jerusalem, King Herod waited and waited, but the wise men did not come back. He realized that they had tricked him, and now he would never find the child they had called the "King of the Jews."

Herod paced around his court, growing even angrier and more determined. Finally he thought of another way to kill the baby he was so afraid of. He gave a cruel and terrible order to his soldiers. He told them to go to Bethlehem and kill every baby boy under two years old.

The guards obeyed. All the boy children in Bethlehem and the hills and coasts around it were murdered because of the king's evil order. But Jesus was safe, far away in Egypt, so Herod's cruelty was for nothing.

Some time later King Herod died. In Egypt, an angel spoke to Joseph in a dream. "Your enemy is dead," he said. "You may go back safely to your homeland."

So Joseph, Mary, and Jesus traveled back to Mary's home in Galilee. There they lived peacefully in the little town of Nazareth, while Jesus grew up.

King Herod orders his soldiers to kill all the baby boys in Bethlehem.

POOR SHEPHERDS AND RICH MEN CAME TO SEE JESUS AND SHARE THE GOOD NEWS OF HIS BIRTH. BUT KING HEROD WAS TOO SELFISH TO REJOICE. ONLY GOD'S GUIDANCE, AND THE OBEDIENCE OF JOSEPH AND THE WISE MEN, KEPT JESUS SAFE.

Mary, Joseph, and Jesus visit Jerusalem for the Passover. They return home after the festival.

On the way home, Mary and Joseph discover that Jesus is missing.

They return to search for him.

Finally, they go to the temple.

There they find Jesus talking with the wise men and answering questions.

Jesus tells Mary and Joseph he is doing his Father's work.

Jesus returns to Nazareth with his parents.

Jesus in the Temple

S THE YEARS WENT BY, JESUS BECAME STRONG, HAPPY, AND WISE, AND FULL OF GOD'S grace. To all their neighbors, Mary, Joseph, and Jesus seemed to be just an ordinary family. Jesus was one of the favorite children in the town.

Each year, with their friends and relations, Mary and Joseph would travel to Jerusalem for the great festival of Passover. It lasted several days, with prayers, celebrations, and feasting. The year that Jesus was twelve years old, they took him along with them on the visit.

When the festival was all over, the family set off on the long journey home, traveling the dusty roads in a big group of friends and relatives, talking and laughing. They had traveled for a whole day before they suddenly realized that Jesus was not with them. Mary and Joseph had been thinking he was with his cousins or some friends; but when they ran to and fro through the group and asked, they realized that no one had seen him all day.

Mary and Joseph were terrified. Their child was lost! Where could he be? They turned back to Jerusalem without resting or stopping, and for three whole days they searched through the city for the missing boy.

At last, desperate with worry, they went to the great temple. There was Jesus. He was sitting in the middle of a group of men, the smartest people in Israel, the wise men and teachers. Jesus was right at home with them, talking and listening and asking questions. The teachers were amazed by how wise he was, and by how well this young boy of twelve understood the difficult things they were discussing.

Jesus' parents were amazed, too, and although they were thankful to find him, they were also a little angry. Mary said, "Oh, my son – how could you have run away like that? Your father and I have been frightened and miserable, searching for you everywhere!"

Jesus looked at them calmly and answered, "Why did you have to search for me? Didn't you know that it was time for me to come to my Father's house, and work at my Father's business?"

He meant that God was his father, and that his real work would be God's work for humankind. But Mary and Joseph did not understand. Jesus came quietly home with them, though, and lived on for many years in Nazareth, obeying his parents. But Mary always remembered that day, and the things Jesus had said.

The whole family returned to Nazareth and Jesus stayed with them there, growing older and wiser.

JESUS WAS A HUMAN BEING, A CHILD IN AN ORDINARY FAMILY; BUT AT THE SAME TIME HE WAS THE SON OF GOD, WHO HAD COME TO EARTH TO SAVE MEN AND WOMEN FROM THEIR SIN AND TO SHOW THEM THE WAY TO HEAVEN.

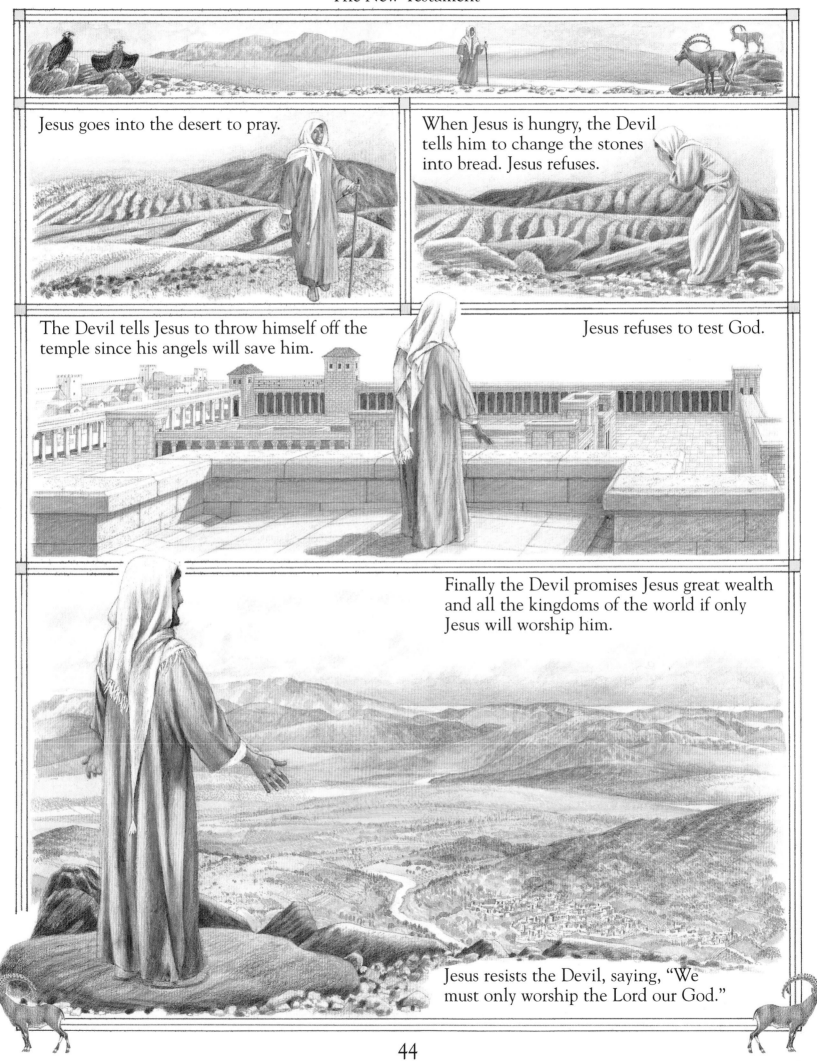

Jesus goes into the desert to pray.

When Jesus is hungry, the Devil tells him to change the stones into bread. Jesus refuses.

The Devil tells Jesus to throw himself off the temple since his angels will save him.

Jesus refuses to test God.

Finally the Devil promises Jesus great wealth and all the kingdoms of the world if only Jesus will worship him.

Jesus resists the Devil, saying, "We must only worship the Lord our God."

The Temptations in the Wilderness

WHEN JESUS WAS ABOUT THIRTY YEARS OLD, HE WENT OFF ALONE INTO A WILD, LONELY PART OF the desert. He went there to pray and to get ready for his work in the world.

For forty days and nights he stayed all alone in the stony wilderness. He saw no one. The only creatures around were the wild beasts and birds of the desert. He talked to no one but God, and slept out on the hard ground.

All the time he was in the wilderness he had nothing to eat and only a little water to drink. So, near the end of this time in the desert, Jesus was very, very hungry.

It was then, when Jesus was weak with hunger, that the Devil came to him and tempted him. First of all he said, "Are you the Son of God? Prove it. If you were really the Son of God you could turn these stones into pieces of bread!"

The thought of bread must have made Jesus feel even hungrier, but he answered, "No. Man does not live on bread alone. We must find strength in the word of God!"

Then the Devil led him to Jerusalem and stood with him on the highest pinnacle of the temple roof. "Come on," he said. "This is a chance to prove you are the Son of God. It says in the holy writings that God will look after His Son, and not even allow Him to trip on a stone. So throw yourself off the roof, Son of God, and the angels will rescue you!"

Jesus just said, "It is also written in the Scriptures, do not try to test the Lord, your God."

The Devil saw he could not make Jesus selfish or proud, so he tried to make him greedy. He took him to the top of a high mountain and showed him the kingdoms of the world in all their glory.

"Now," he said, "I will give you all these lands. I will let you

Jesus spends forty days and forty nights praying to God.

have all these beautiful, rich, powerful kingdoms for yourself. The whole world can be yours, on one condition. I will give it all to you if you will just kneel down and worship me!"

Then in a terrible voice, Jesus cried, "Get away from me, Satan! It is written in the holy book that we must worship the Lord our God faithfully, and serve only Him."

The Devil knew that he was finally beaten and so vanished in a terrible fury. When he had gone, angels came to Jesus, and gave him food to eat.

Jesus was now ready to start his work in the world. He returned to Galilee and traveled around, teaching people in the synagogues and preaching the good news about God and his kingdom. These people were amazed at his words and praised God.

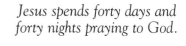

THE DEVIL KNEW THAT IT IS VERY HARD TO RESIST TEMPTATION WHEN YOU ARE HUNGRY AND LONELY. BUT JESUS REMAINED STRONG, AND DID NOT GIVE IN TO THE DEVIL'S INVITATIONS OF FOOD AND POWER.

Jesus travels around with his disciples, spreading the word of God.

Jesus, Mary, and the disciples attend a wedding feast in Cana.

When the wine runs out, Mary asks Jesus to help.

Jesus tells a servant to fill six stone jars with water.

The servants serve the chief steward.

The chief steward drinks and is surprised that the host has saved the best wine until now.

The servants are astonished that the water has turned to wine.

The Wedding at Cana

SOON IT WOULD BE TIME FOR JESUS TO BEGIN HIS WORK ON EARTH. GOD HAD SENT HIS SON INTO THE world so that people would believe in Him and come and live with Him in Heaven.

Jesus chose twelve disciples to help him, and together they traveled around the land of Galilee. There were Peter and Andrew, two brothers who were fishermen; their friends, James and John; and Matthew, who saw Jesus one day and left his job as a tax-collector to follow him. The others were called Philip, Bartholomew, Thomas, James, Thaddaeus, Simon, and Judas.

One day they were all invited to a wedding in a town called Cana, and Jesus' mother Mary was with them.

At that time, very few people knew about Jesus. They certainly did not know that he was the Son of God and could do great things. He sat quietly among the ordinary guests.

During the feast much wine was drunk. Mary noticed that the jars of wine were almost empty. She wanted to save the host from being embarrassed, and she had great faith in her son, so she whispered to Jesus, "There is no more wine."

Jesus did not make any promises. He turned to his mother and said,

Mary tells the servants to do whatever Jesus tells them.

"My time has not yet come."

Mary still believed that Jesus would help. Privately, she said to the servants at the feast, "Do whatever he tells you."

After a moment, Jesus called a servant to him and pointed at six huge stone water jars that were standing in the corner. He said, "Fill those jars with water," and the servants did, although they wondered why.

When the enormous jars had been filled to the brim, Jesus said to them, "Now pour some into a jug and take it to the steward in charge of the wedding feast. Let him taste it."

The servants did as they were told, still wondering what this was about. But when they poured the chief steward a drink, they saw that it was not water any longer, but wine.

When the chief steward drank from his cup, he was astonished. He did not know where this new wine had come from, but he realized it was very good. He said to the bridegroom, "Most people serve the good wine first, then bring out the worst later. But you saved the best for last!"

The chief steward and the bridegroom did not know what had happened, but the servants knew and marveled at it, and the disciples knew and put their faith in Jesus.

So the party went on, with great merriment, and Mary was happy that her son had helped.

THIS WAS THE FIRST MIRACLE THAT JESUS DID, AT AN ORDINARY WEDDING IN THE SMALL TOWN OF CANA. IT SHOWED HIS POWER AND GLORY AND MADE THE DISCIPLES BELIEVE IN HIM EVEN MORE STRONGLY.

Friends bring a paralyzed man to Jesus. They lower him through a hole in the roof.

Jesus tells the man to get up and walk. He is healed!

Later, Jesus and the disciples set out to sea in a small boat, but a terrible storm springs up.

The disciples are terrified. They wake Jesus up and beg him to save them.

Jesus stretches his hands out over the waves and says, "Peace, be still!"

Right away, the wind drops and the sea becomes calm.

Three Miracles

JESUS STARTED TO TRAVEL FAR AND WIDE ACROSS THE LAND, TEACHING PEOPLE ABOUT THE Kingdom of God. Sometimes people with terrible illnesses begged him for help. On one of these occasions, Jesus stretched out his hand and cured a man with leprosy, whose skin was covered in such terrible sores that people were afraid to touch him.

Another time, Jesus was in a house packed with eager followers. Some people came to see him, carrying a friend who was paralyzed and could not move. They could not get through the crowd, because there were so many people there, so four of them climbed onto the roof, made a hole in it, and lowered their sick friend down on ropes, right in front of Jesus.

Jesus was impressed by their faith and he said to the man, "Get up, take your mat, and go home." The man stood up, and everyone saw that he was healed. These miracles and others amazed people and made them believe in Jesus, and praise the power of God.

One day, Jesus had been teaching and telling stories beside the Sea of Galilee, and in the evening, although they were all tired, he said to his disciples, "We must cross to the other side, to the land of the Gadarenes."

They set out to sea in a small fishing boat, with other small boats following them. Jesus was so weary that he fell asleep, with his head on a cushion, in the stern of the boat.

But as the night grew darker, a great wind rose up. The wind howled and battered the sea, and big waves tossed the little boat around and began to slop into it, filling it up with water. The disciples were afraid that it would sink. The wind blew even harder. Terrified, they woke Jesus, shouting, "Master, Master, we're going to die – don't you care that we are about to die? Save us!"

Jesus woke up, yawning. He stood up and turned to the disciples saying, "Why are you afraid? Don't you have any faith in God?" Then he stretched out his hands, and told the winds, "Be quiet," and told the waves, "Peace, be still!"

At that moment the wind dropped, the sea heaved for a moment and became flat, everything went quiet, and there was a great calm. A few minutes before, the little boat had been struggling in the storm. Now it floated on the water, rocking gently.

The disciples forgot about being cold and wet and looked at each other in amazement, their hearts filled with fear and wonder. "What sort of man is this?" They said to one another. "Even the wind and the sea obey him!"

Jesus falls asleep in the boat and even a strong wind does not wake him.

JESUS PERFORMED MANY MIRACLES. HIS MIRACLES WERE A SIGN THAT GOD WAS WORKING THROUGH JESUS HIS SON, GIVING HIM AUTHORITY OVER NATURE AND THE DEVIL, AND GIVING HIM THE POWER TO FORGIVE SINS.

Jesus the Storyteller

NEWS OF JESUS' TEACHING HAD SPREAD, AND WHEREVER HE WENT, GREAT CROWDS OF PEOPLE CAME to see him. He often told them stories to help them understand about God and how He wants us to live. These stories are called parables.

This is the parable of the lost son. Once there was a rich farmer, who had two sons. The youngest son spoke to his father, saying, "Father,

The youngest son wastes all his money and has to take a job feeding pigs.

give me my share of the family wealth." So the father divided his money between his two sons.

The youngest son went off to a distant country, and wasted all the money he had. In the end he had nothing left, and the only work he could find was feeding pigs. He was so hungry that he wanted to eat the pigs' food.

This made him ashamed. The young man thought, "Even the servants at my father's house have bread to eat! I will go back and tell my father that I am sorry, and ask him if I can be one of his servants."

Long before the son got home, his father saw him coming and ran out to hug and kiss him.

The son said, "Father, I am sorry. I have sinned against you and against God. I am not worthy to be called your son." But the father was so pleased to see his son again that he called his servants to bring him fine clothes and to kill the best, fattest calf for dinner.

The elder brother heard the music and dancing from the feast as he came back, tired from his day's work. When he saw why his father was celebrating he was very angry, and wouldn't come indoors.

His father came out of the party to find his eldest son, who said bitterly, "Father, I have worked faithfully for you all these years, but you've never given me anything. My lazy brother has wasted your money enjoying himself, and now that he's come back you've prepared him this great feast. It's not fair."

The father said, "Son, you are always with me, and everything I have is yours. But we must be merry and glad, because your brother was dead and is alive; he was lost, and is found."

Jesus told this story to show that God is a loving Father. He will always forgive us when we have done something wrong, however wicked we have been, as long as we are really sorry and turn back to him.

The son decides to return and ask his father to forgive him. As he approaches, his father runs out to welcome him home.

Another of Jesus' parables was about an unforgiving servant. One of the King's servants owed him a lot of money, but couldn't pay. "Well," said the King, "In that case, I shall sell you as a slave, and your wife and children, too."

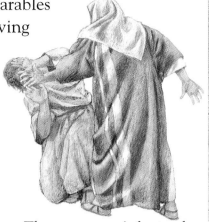

The servant won't forgive the man who owes him money.

The servant begged, "Lord King, have patience. I will pay back what I owe." The King felt sorry for him, and let him off.

But later, the same servant met a man who owed him a small amount of money. He grabbed him and said, "Pay up, now!" The poor man begged for mercy, but the servant had no patience and threw him into prison.

When the King heard about this he was angry. He said, "O, you wicked man. I let you off because you begged me to. You should have had pity on your fellow servant, as I had pity on you!" And threw the servant into prison.

Jesus sternly told the people, "God will do the same to you. He cannot forgive you unless you forgive each other."

Not all the parables were about forgiveness. One day, Jesus told the story of a master, who left three servants to look after his property. He gave each of them some coins called talents. A talent was more than they could earn in ten years.

The first servant got five talents, the second got two talents, and the third servant got one talent. The first went out and traded his five talents until he had twice that amount. The man with two did the same. But the man with only one talent just buried it in the ground.

When the master returned, the first servant brought ten talents back to his master, and the second brought four. "Well done, faithful servants!" said the master, praising them for having made the most of what they were given.

Then the third servant dug up his one talent and gave it to his master saying, "Master, I was afraid of being in trouble if I lost the talent, so I buried it. Here it is. I'm giving it back to you."

The master said, "You lazy, wicked servant! At least you should have put the money in the bank and earned interest! Give it to my hard-working servant who has ten coins, and go away!"

Listening to Jesus' story, people understood that God wants us to use all the gifts that He has given us, and not to be lazy or waste them.

The master is angry with the servant who has done nothing with his money.

JESUS TOLD PARABLES TO TEACH PEOPLE ABOUT GOD IN A WAY THAT THEY WOULD UNDERSTAND AND REMEMBER. THESE STORIES SHOW US WHAT GOD IS LIKE AND HOW HE WANTS US TO LIVE OUR LIVES.

Jesus teaches the crowd and heals sick people.

A huge crowd follows Jesus to a hillside.

The disciples tell Jesus to send the crowd away, since they have nothing to eat.

The only food they can find is five loaves and two fish.

Jesus blesses the food, and the disciples hand it out to the crowd.

The more food they hand out, the more there is. Everyone has plenty to eat.

There are twelve baskets full of leftovers.

Jesus Feeds the Five Thousand

EVERYONE WAS TALKING ABOUT THE AMAZING THINGS THAT JESUS DID AND SAID, SO EVERYWHERE he went, more and more people followed him. Jesus listened to their troubles, healed the sick, and taught them about God's kingdom.

One day Jesus wanted to spend a little time away from the crowds, so he traveled to the shores of the Sea of Galilee and climbed up a hill to sit down quietly for a while with his disciples. But, as usual, a great crowd of people followed him.

Many of the people had brought their friends and relations who were ill. They struggled up the hill carrying children, the lame, and injured people, and leading the blind, and brought them all to Jesus.

He was filled with pity for the people and could not turn them away; so he prayed for them and healed them. When people saw this they praised God, with joy in their hearts, and it became a great, happy meeting by the shores of the Sea of Galilee.

Throughout the day, more and more people came close to Jesus, talked with him, and listened to his stories.

By the evening, no one had any food left to eat. The disciples said to Jesus, "Send the people

People bring sick children to Jesus and he heals them.

away, so that they can go to the villages nearby and find food."

Jesus wanted to see how much they trusted in his power. "You feed them," he said.

The disciples did not understand what he meant. They pointed at the great crowd. There were thousands upon thousands of men, women, and children. They said to Jesus, "How can we feed them all? There are too many! It would take eight months' pay to buy enough bread."

Jesus just said, "Well, how much food is there? Go and see."

The disciples searched high and low, but all they could find was a boy who had five loaves of barley bread and two little salted fish. They brought him to Jesus.

"Good," said Jesus. He told all the people to sit down on the grass. He took the boy's five loaves and the two fish, and looking up to Heaven, gave thanks to God. Then he said, "Give the food out."

The disciples, wondering what would happen, began handing out the bread and fish. But, to their amazement, the more food they gave out, the more food there was.

In the end there was enough food to make a good meal for more than five thousand people on that rocky hillside by the sea, and when everyone was finished there were twelve baskets full of leftovers.

So the people went away, full of strength, and praising God.

JESUS WATCHED OVER HIS FOLLOWERS AND CARED FOR THEM. THE MIRACLE OF THE LOAVES AND FISH SHOWED THE PEOPLE THAT, EVEN WHEN IT SEEMS IMPOSSIBLE, GOD CAN TAKE CARE OF US.

Jesus teaches Mary, while her sister Martha does the housework.

Jesus tells Martha not to worry about her work, but to listen to him.

The sisters send Jesus a message that their brother is ill.

When Jesus arrives, Martha tells him that Lazarus has already died.

The two sisters take Jesus to the tomb where Lazarus is buried.

When the tomb has been opened, Jesus calls to Lazarus to come out.

Lazarus walks out of the tomb in his white wrappings, alive!

Martha, Mary, and Lazarus

THERE WAS A VILLAGE CALLED BETHANY, NOT FAR FROM JERUSALEM, IN JUDEA. ONE DAY, JESUS visited two sisters here, named Martha and Mary. While he and his disciples were in the house, Martha bustled around looking after everyone and serving the food.

But Mary just sat down at Jesus' feet, listening to his teaching. After a while, Martha grew angry with her sister, and asked Jesus to tell Mary to get up and help with the housework. Gently, Jesus said, "No, Martha. It is more important to listen to the word of God than always to be busy with work."

Martha, Mary, and their brother, Lazarus, became good friends of Jesus. A little while later, when Jesus had left Judea, the women sent him a desperate message. It said that Lazarus was very ill, and asked Jesus to come and heal him.

Jesus stayed where he was for two days longer and then said to his disciples, "We shall go back to Bethany. Our friend Lazarus is dead, but I shall bring him back to life."

When they arrived, they found that Lazarus had already been buried in a tomb, and many friends had come from Jerusalem to comfort the sisters.

When Jesus arrived, Martha said, "Lord, if you had been here, my brother would not have died. God will do anything you ask."

Jesus said to Martha, "Your brother will rise again."

"Yes," said Martha sadly. "I know he will rise again at the end of the world. Everybody will." She believed that one day all the dead would be brought back to life.

But Jesus said, "I am the way for people to live again. No one who believes in me will ever really die. Show me where Lazarus is buried."

The two sisters and their friends took him to the cave where Lazarus's body had been put. Jesus wept to see it. Then he ordered the people to push away the stone from the opening of the tomb. Martha was horrified and said to Jesus, "Lord, he has been dead for four days. The body will smell!"

Jesus just replied, "I have told you before that if you believe, you will see the glory of God."

Jesus prayed to his Father in Heaven. The people by the grave were afraid and wondered what would happen, but they trusted Jesus. Strong men rolled away the stone from the dark opening and Jesus cried out in a loud voice, "Lazarus, come out!"

The dead man came out, still in his white wrappings from the grave. Lazarus had come back to life! Many of the people who saw this miracle began to believe that Jesus really was the Son of God.

When Jesus sees Lazarus's tomb, he weeps.

JESUS RAISED LAZARUS TO SHOW THAT GOD IS ALL POWERFUL, AND HAS AUTHORITY OVER EVERYTHING. THIS MIRACLE ALSO GAVE A FORETASTE OF JESUS' OWN RISING FROM THE DEAD AT EASTER.

Jesus arrives in Jerusalem riding on a donkey.

One of the disciples, Judas, agrees to help the chief priests capture Jesus.

Before the Passover meal, Jesus washes his disciples' feet.

At supper, Jesus tells the disciples that one of them will betray him that night.

Judas knows that Jesus is talking about him, and leaves.

Jesus goes to Gethsemane to pray. He asks the disciples to stay awake with him, but they fall asleep.

Judas arrives with a group of soldiers.

The Last Supper

**J**ESUS ARRIVED IN JERUSALEM FOR THE PASSOVER

FEAST RIDING ON A DONKEY. HUGE CROWDS of people gathered to welcome him. They sang and shouted, and cut palm leaves from the trees to lay in his path.

But Jesus had enemies, too. Priests and other important people were afraid that he had come to take power from them. They wanted to get rid of Jesus. One of the disciples, Judas Iscariot, went to the chief priests and offered to hand Jesus over to them. They agreed to pay him thirty pieces of silver.

Jesus knew that the time of his death had almost come. He told the disciples that they would all eat the holy Passover meal together. When they sat down, Jesus put a towel around his waist, poured water into a bowl, and knelt before each of the twelve men to wash their feet, which were dusty from the journey.

Peter was shocked that Jesus was doing this. "Why, Lord?" he asked.

Jesus said, "I am your Master. But I have washed your feet as an example, to show how you must all help and serve one another."

Later Jesus looked sadly at his companions. "One of you will betray me tonight," he said.

The disciples were horrified. They looked at one another and said, "Who could he mean?"

"It is the one to whom I give bread," said Jesus quietly. He gave a piece of bread to Judas and said, "Do what you have to do, quickly." Judas went out into the dark, alone.

During the meal, Jesus took the bread, gave a prayer of thanks, broke the bread into pieces and gave it to the disciples saying, "Take this and eat it, it is my body." Then he poured out some wine and gave it to them saying, "Drink this, it is my blood. Do this in memory of me."

After supper, Jesus went with his disciples to a garden called Gethsemane. "Stay with me, wait with me," said Jesus. "My heart is full of sorrow tonight." And he knelt down weeping, and prayed to God. "Father, please take this suffering away from me," he prayed. "But let your will be done, not mine."

The disciples, weary from the journey and the supper, fell asleep. Jesus woke them. "Stay awake with me for one hour," he asked. Twice again they fell asleep while he prayed. At last Jesus said, "Never mind. The hour has come. The traitor is here!" Judas was coming toward them, leading soldiers with swords, clubs, and burning torches.

At the meal, Jesus blesses the bread and wine and shares it with his disciples.

ALL OVER THE WORLD CHRISTIANS STILL MEET TOGETHER TO REMEMBER THE LAST SUPPER THAT JESUS SHARED WITH HIS FRIENDS. THEY EAT BREAD AND DRINK WINE TO REMEMBER HOW JESUS GAVE HIS BODY AND BLOOD TO SAVE US ALL.

The soldiers come to arrest Jesus.

Jesus is taken to the chief priests, who question him.

Pilate asks the crowd whether he should free Jesus, but they shout, "Crucify him!"

Jesus is dressed as a king, with a crown of thorns.

Jesus carries the cross to Calvary.

Jesus is nailed to the cross and crucified along with two thieves.

The soldiers take Jesus' clothes and divide them between them.

The Crucifixion

WHEN THEY CAME TO SEIZE JESUS, PETER DREW HIS SWORD AND CUT OFF A SERVANT'S EAR. JESUS SAID, "Put away your sword! If my Father wanted to save me, He could send an army of angels!" He touched the servant's head, and healed him. As the soldiers arrested Jesus, the disciples ran away.

Jesus was taken to the chief priest. "Are you the Son of God?" asked Caiaphas, the High Priest.

"I am," Jesus answered. Caiaphas shouted, "What more proof do we need? He should die! It is a sin to say you are the Son of God."

Then the priests took him to Pontius Pilate, the governor. Pilate could see that Jesus was innocent, but decided not to interfere. He gave the people one last chance to save Jesus. It was the custom to set one prisoner free to celebrate the Passover. There was a murderer in the prison called Barabbas, so Pilate asked the crowd, "Who shall I set free? Jesus or Barabbas?"

Jesus' enemies shouted, "Barabbas!"

So Pilate asked, "What shall I do with Jesus?"

"Crucify him!" the people cried.

The governor was afraid of trouble, so he handed Jesus over to them, even though he knew that Jesus was innocent.

So the soldiers took Jesus away, pulled off his clothes, and made fun of him by dressing him up as

As Jesus dies, darkness falls, although it is still day.

a king. They pressed a crown made of thorns on his head and spat at him. They slapped him, and laughed at him saying, "Hail, King of the Jews!"

Then they dressed Jesus in his own clothes and made him carry a heavy wooden cross up a hill called Calvary. It was a long road, and Jesus was weak from their cruelty. At last they reached the top of the hill. The soldiers set up the cross, and nailed Jesus to it by his hands and feet. Then they divided his clothes between them.

There were two thieves on crosses next to Jesus. One of them shouted, "If you are really the Son of God, save yourself. And us!" But the other thief believed in Jesus, and said, "We deserve to die for what we did, but he has done nothing wrong." He said to Jesus, "Lord, remember me when you enter your Kingdom."

Jesus answered the thief, "Believe me, this very day you will be with me in Heaven."

As the day went on, Jesus grew weaker. Once, he spoke and said, "Father, forgive them. They don't know what they are doing." Another time, in great pain, he cried, "My God, my God, why have you abandoned me?"

At last, he said, "Father, into your hands I place my soul," and died. Although it was midday, darkness fell. A soldier exclaimed, "This man really was the Son of God."

Jesus' mother, his disciple John, and some of Jesus' women followers were there and saw all that happened.

JESUS WAS GOD'S SON. HE WANTED TO SHARE COMPLETELY IN ALL THAT WE HAVE TO EXPERIENCE, INCLUDING SUFFERING AND DEATH. HE WAS SINLESS, BUT HE KNEW THAT IT WAS ONLY BY HIS DEATH THAT OUR SINS COULD BE FORGIVEN.

The Resurrection

SADLY, JESUS' FRIENDS TOOK HIS BODY, WRAPPED IT IN CLEAN WHITE LINEN CLOTHS, AND LAID IT carefully in a tomb. It was a newly made cave, and they closed the entrance with an enormous stone so that no harm could come to Jesus' body from robbers or wild beasts.

The chief priests were worried, too. They went to the governor, Pontius Pilate, and said, "We must guard that tomb. This man once told his followers that he was going to rise from the dead after three days. They might come and steal the body, then pretend he has come back to life. It could cause a lot of trouble."

"Take a guard and make the tomb secure," said Pilate. So they sealed up the entrance, and put soldiers on guard outside.

On the third day, very early in the morning, Mary Magdalene and a friend came to the tomb. They hoped to put precious ointment and better wrappings on the body, because of their love for Jesus. When they got there, they were terrified to see that the enormous stone had been rolled aside and the tomb was empty. They looked at the place where Jesus' dead body had been laid, and saw that it was gone.

Mary Magdalene ran and found two of the disciples. "He is gone!" she said. "Someone has

Mary Magdalene meets Jesus outside the empty tomb. He has risen from the dead!

taken Jesus' body, and I don't know where they have laid him."

They ran back to the tomb with her. One of the disciples was Peter; he looked into the tomb and saw the linen cloths the body had been wrapped in lying there. The two disciples went off to tell the others. But Mary stayed by the tomb, weeping.

She looked in again at the place where the body had been, and suddenly she saw two angels in white sitting there. They said to her, "Woman, why are you crying? He is risen."

Then another voice said, "Why are you weeping? Who are you looking for?"

Mary thought it was the gardener, and said through her tears, "Sir, if you have taken his body away, please tell me where."

The man said, "Mary!" and she turned and saw that it was Jesus himself, alive. Great joy filled her heart.

That evening, the disciples met in a room with locked doors. Suddenly Jesus appeared in the room, saying, "Peace be with you." He showed them his hands, where the nails had been hammered through them, and the wound in his side. The disciples could not believe at first that Jesus was real and not a ghost. So Jesus asked for food, and they gave him some fish and he ate it.

Then he solemnly said to them, "Peace be with you. My Father sent me, and now I send you out into the world."

The disciples that saw Jesus believed that he had

truly risen from the dead. But one of the twelve, Thomas, was not with them in the room when Jesus came. Later, when the others told him that Jesus was alive again, he refused to believe them. Thomas said, "I won't believe it until I see the mark of the nails in his hands and touch the wound in his side."

Thomas touches the wounds in Jesus' hands and side and believes that Jesus is alive again.

A week later, when the disciples met again, Thomas was with them. Again, even though all the doors were locked, Jesus came and stood among them and said, "Peace be with you!" He called Thomas over and said, "Put out your finger, feel my hands, put your hand in the wound in my side. Have faith: believe!"

Thomas said, "My Lord and my God!"

And Jesus answered, "Thomas, you have seen me and believed, but those people who have not seen me and still believe are more blessed."

Jesus appeared to his disciples on other occasions. Once, he showed himself at the Sea of Tiberias, when some of them were fishing. He told them to cast their nets on the other side of the boat, and suddenly they caught lots of fish.

Jesus made a fire, and gave them bread, and they cooked the fish together and ate it.

Jesus spoke to the disciples, telling them to go out into the world and tell everyone what they had seen and what they believed, and to baptize all those who had faith. Jesus told them that he had to return to Heaven, but he would send the Holy Spirit to help them carry on God's work. The Holy Spirit would be in everyone who believed, giving them the power to do all the things that God wanted them to do.

After Jesus had finished speaking, he was lifted into the air and vanished on a bright cloud. The disciples never saw him on earth again.

But while they looked up at the sky, two angels came and said, "Jesus will come back to you one day, in the same way that you have seen him taken up into Heaven."

That was the end of Jesus' time on earth. But for his followers, it was the beginning of their work. Many people joined them and the church grew quickly. The twelve disciples became the first Christian teachers, traveling around to bring everybody the good news about Jesus, the Son of God, who came to save the world.

Jesus appears to the disciples while they are fishing on the Sea of Tiberias.

AFTER JESUS LEFT HIS DISCIPLES AND WENT TO HEAVEN, HE SENT HIS HOLY SPIRIT TO CONTINUE TO GUIDE ALL THOSE WHO BELIEVE IN HIM. ONE DAY, ALL THOSE WHO TRUST IN GOD WILL JOIN HIM IN HEAVEN.

Who's Who in the Bible

THE OLD TESTAMENT

Aaron *Pages 23, 25*
Moses' brother. He helped Moses lead the Israelites out of Egypt.

Adam *Pages 10–13*
The first man, and husband of Eve. Adam and Eve disobeyed God. Because of this they were thrown out of Paradise.

Daniel *Pages 32–33*
An Israelite who became an important official in Babylon. His faith in God saved him when he was thrown into a den of lions.

Darius *Pages 32–33*
The King of Babylon who had Daniel thrown into the lions' den.

David *Pages 28–29*
One of the first Kings of Israel. When David was a boy, he killed the giant Philistine, Goliath, and won a victory for the Israelites.

Delilah *Pages 26–27*
The woman who tricked Samson into revealing the secret of his strength and betrayed him to the Philistines.

Eve *Pages 10–13*
The first woman, and the wife of Adam. Eve was deceived by the serpent and ate the forbidden fruit from the Tree of Knowledge.

Goliath *Pages 28–29*
A giant Philistine. David killed him with a sling.

Jacob *Pages 16–19*
The father of Joseph and of eleven other sons. Later, God named Jacob "Israel." The Israelites were the descendants of Jacob and his sons.

Jesse *Page 29*
The father of David.

Jonah *Pages 34–35*
An Israelite prophet. When God told Jonah to go to Nineveh he refused and ran away to sea. He was thrown overboard and swallowed by a fish before he realized that he had been wrong to turn away from God.

Joseph *Pages 16–19*
Jacob's favorite son. His brothers were jealous of him, and sold him as a slave. He lived in Egypt for years before becoming the Pharaoh's chief minister. He helped Egypt survive a famine and saved his family.

Moses' mother hides him in the bulrushes.

Moses *Pages 20–25*
A leader of the Israelites. Moses' mother hid him in the bulrushes, where he was found by Pharaoh's daughter. He was brought up as an Egyptian, but later, God called him to lead the Israelites out of slavery in Egypt and into the Promised Land.

Noah *Pages 14–15*
When God sent a flood to wash the world clean of wickedness, Noah and his family took refuge in the ark and were the only people saved.

Samson *Pages 26–27*
An Israelite who had great strength. Delilah betrayed Samson to his enemies, the Philistines. They blinded him and threw him in prison, but Samson got his revenge.

Solomon *Pages 30–31*
King of Israel and son of King David. Solomon was famous for his wisdom.

Adam and Eve

David

Joseph and his brothers

Noah and his wife

THE NEW TESTAMENT

Caiaphas *Page 59*
The High Priest at the time of Jesus' arrest. Caiaphas questioned Jesus before he was crucified.

Disciples *Pages 46–47 onward*
Jesus' twelve followers: Peter, Andrew, James, John, Bartholomew, Philip, Thomas, Matthew, James, Thaddeus, Simon, and Judas Iscariot.

Elizabeth *Pages 38–39*
Mary's cousin. Mary visited Elizabeth while she was pregnant and found that Elizabeth was pregnant too.

Gabriel *Pages 38–39*
The angel who told Mary that she was going to have a baby, Jesus.

Herod *Pages 40–41*
The King of Judea. He had all the baby boys in Bethlehem put to death when he heard that a new king, Jesus, had been born.

Jesus Christ *The New Testament*
The Son of God. God loved the world so much that He sent Jesus to live on Earth and tell people about the Kingdom of Heaven. Jesus performed miracles, and healed many people. He was sentenced to death and crucified, but after three days he rose from the dead.

Joseph *Pages 38–43*
The husband of Mary. He was a carpenter from Nazareth.

Judas Iscariot *Pages 47, 56–57*
One of Jesus' twelve disciples. Judas betrayed Jesus to the chief priests for thirty pieces of silver. He later killed himself.

Jesus with Martha and Mary

Lazarus *Pages 54–55*
The brother of Martha and Mary and one of Jesus' friends. Lazarus fell ill and died, but Jesus raised him from the dead.

Martha *Pages 54–55*
The sister of Lazarus and Mary, and one of Jesus' close friends.

Mary *Pages 38–47, 59*
The mother of Jesus and Joseph's wife. She was a young girl in Nazareth when the Angel Gabriel told her that she would be the mother of Jesus. She married Joseph.

Mary *Pages 54–55*
The sister of Lazarus and Martha, and one of Jesus' close friends.

Mary Magdalene *Page 60*
One of Jesus' followers. On Easter morning, Mary went on her own to Jesus' tomb and became the first person to see Jesus after he had risen from the dead.

Peter *Pages 47, 57, 59, 60*
A fisherman and one of Jesus' twelve disciples. He was originally named Simon, but Jesus renamed him Peter, which means "the rock," because of his strong faith.

Pontius Pilate *Pages 58–60*
The Roman governor of Judea. Jesus was brought to him for questioning and Pilate sentenced him to be crucified.

Thomas *Pages 47, 61*
One of the twelve disciples. He is often called "Doubting Thomas," because at first he did not believe that Jesus had risen from the dead.

Wise men *Pages 40–41*
Men from the East who saw a new star appear in the sky when Jesus was born. The star led them to Jesus. The Bible does not say how many wise men there were, but many people think there were three because they brought three gifts.

Jesus heals a blind man.

Peter

Joseph and Mary

The three wise men

Index

Acknowledgments
Dorling Kindersley would like to thank the
following people for their help: Dom Benedict
Sankey, Jacqueline Gooden, Adrienne Hutchinson.